SELF-PORTRAIT: TRINA SCHART HYMAN

SELF-PORTRAIT:

Trina Schart Hyman

written and illustrated by
Trina Schart Hyman

⏶

Addison-Wesley

FOR KATRIN AND MICHAEL... WHO ONCE UPON A TIME WERE WALTZING. GRACEFULLY, SLOWLY, SWIFTLY. TURNING WITH THE WIND AS PEOPLE DANCE IN A DREAM. THEY WERE ICE SKATING ON THE POND UNDER A SKY FULL OF BRILLIANT STARS. THE WINTER STARLIGHT SHONE ON THEIR FLYING HAIR; HIS WHITE-GOLD, AND HERS FIRE BLACK. THEY LAUGHED AND TURNED and SWIRLED TOGETHER. KATRIN WAS WEARING HER SILKY PANDA NIGHTGOWN, AND MICHAEL WAS WEARING HIS BEST SUIT. IT WAS FORTY DEGREES BELOW ZERO, AND THE STARS CAME DOWN ONE BY ONE TO WALTZ WITH THEM... TSH.1981

Text Copyright © 1981 by Trina Schart Hyman
Illustrations Copyright © 1981 by Trina Schart Hyman
All Rights Reserved
Addison Wesley Publishing Company, Inc.
Reading, Massachusetts 01867
Printed in the United States of America

ABCDEFGHIJK-WZ-8987654321

Library of Congress Cataloging in Publication Data
Hyman, Trina Schart,
   Self-portrait, Trina Schart Hyman.
   (Self-portrait collection)
   SUMMARY: A well-known illustrator of children's
books discusses her life and art.
   1. Hyman, Trina Schart,   —Juvenile
literature.   2.   Illustrators—United States—
Biography—Juvenile literature. 3.   Illustrated
books, Children's—Juvenile literature. [1. Hyman,
Trina Schart,   2.   Illustrators]
I. Title. II. Series.
NC975.5.H93A2 1981   741.64′2′0924 [B] [92]
ISBN 0-201-09308-1   80-26662

A WALK TO THE FARM TO BUY EGGS, IN 1942

THE FARM

I was born forty-two years ago in Philadelphia, Pennsylvania. We lived in a rural area about twenty miles north of the city. Our house was in one of the very first housing "developments" built during the Second World War. It was a little square brick house on a corner of new green grass. My father planted a tiny weeping willow tree and a golden ash in the front lawn, and my mother made a big garden in the backyard.

Those six blocks of little houses were out of place in the landscape, which at that time was open, grassy fields, some dense patches of woods, hidden rocky streams, and just a few old houses— houses with lawns so richly green and soft, and trees so big and gnarled and ancient that I knew they all belonged rightfully in their places and that we did not really belong, yet, in ours.

The farm was the oldest of the old places. It was set back from the road, and although you could see it from the

corner of our yard, you had to walk the length of two fields and then down a long avenue of giant elms and old fierce boxwood trees before you could get to the house. It was a long, low, rambling stone and stucco farmhouse with at least forty rooms and three chimneys and a slate roof. It had an enormous stone barn, a mossy spring house, a romantic hidden rock garden, several flower gardens, an enormous and businesslike vegetable garden, and a lovely pond fed by ancient springs. It had horses, cows, three kinds of chickens, geese, sheep, and goats, and lots of dogs and cats. The barn was always filled with hay; a dark, sweet, dusty landscape that reached four stories high. The deep, rich smell of animals and manure and drying clover was so thick it seemed touchable, like velvet. The people who owned the farm were the King and Queen to me.

The Queen wore farmers' overalls, heavy laced boots, faded flannel shirts, an old manure-stained sailor's hat, and beautiful old rings set with magic stones on her long fingers. She was always darkly tanned as a gypsy. She had an elegant bony face and a fierce smile with long white teeth. She was an artist, and she painted portraits of people who were as mysterious as she.

One of the first drawings I can remember working on was of the Queen with a big basket of eggs on her arm. I didn't think her overalls were pretty, so I drew her in an elaborate long dress with lots of little egg-shaped polka dots.

I SHOW THE QUEEN MY DRAWING.

I never saw the King, but I learned later that he was a gentleman farmer and an archeologist who spent most of his time in faraway, exotic countries.

In the winter, we skated on the farm's pond. Everybody went—all the moms and dads and kids and everybody's dogs. Usually someone built a little bonfire at the far edge of the pond, and sometimes the Queen would come trudging through the snow with a huge coffeepot full of hot chocolate. It seemed then that it was always the week before Christmas, the sky was full of snowflakes ready to fall, and angels were perched on the barn along with the pigeons.

One spring, years later, when I was in art school, the farm was sold, and men and machines came and tore it down. They ripped up the grand old elms and boxwoods and burned them in a big fire. They smashed the old stone and stucco walls and splintered the hand-painted blue and white Dutch tiles that lined the fireplaces. They shattered the fragile wavery-gold and violet-tinted glass of the windows. They burned the golden planks of the floors and the giant oak beams of the ceilings. They battered on the solid old barn, with its families of rats and pigeons and swallows, until it finally collapsed and died; then they plowed it under with their bulldozers.

I learned something, that day. I learned that everything changes, and nothing is safe. I still have dreams about the farm. It was my first kingdom, and in a way, my first real home.

As I grew up, the days of the King and Queen came to an end. They spent less and less time at the farm, and finally the farm and its gardens were left to collect dust and weeds and dream away the days.

YOU CAN'T GO HOME NOW, EVER.   1957

LITTLE RED RIDING HOOD

I was a really strange little kid. I was born terrified of anything and everything that moved or spoke. I was afraid of people, especially. All people—kids my own age, all grownups, even my own family. Dogs (until my parents bought me a puppy of my own), horses, trees, grass, cars, streets. I was afraid of the stars and the wind. Who knows why?

My mother is a beautiful woman with red hair and the piercing blue gaze of a hawk. She never seemed afraid of anyone or anything. It was she who gave me the courage to draw and a love of books. She read to me from the time I was a baby, and once, when I was three or four and she was reading my favorite story, the words on the page, her spoken words, and the scenes in my head fell together in a blinding flash. I could read!

The story was *Little Red Riding Hood,* and it was so much a part of me that I actually became Little Red Riding Hood. My mother sewed me a red satin cape with a hood that I wore almost every day, and on those days, she would make me a "basket of goodies" to take to my grandmother's house. (My only grandmother lived in Rhode Island, three hundred miles away, but that didn't matter.) I'd take the basket and carefully negotiate the backyard, "going to Grandmother's house." My dog, Tippy, was the wolf. Whenever we met, which in a small backyard had to be fairly often, there was an intense confrontation. My father was the woodsman, and I greeted him when he came home each day with relief and joy.

I was Red Riding Hood for a year or more. I think it's a great tribute to my mother that she never gave up and took me to a psychiatrist, and if she ever worried, she has never let me know.

MY FATHER AND THE MUSEUM

My father worked as a plumbing and heating supplies salesman. He loved music and singing, walking quietly in the woods, and fly-fishing. He could play almost any musical instrument, but the one he played most often was a concertina-accordian, with inlaid mother-of-pearl and wood designs on it. He played the harmonica, too, and sometimes he played both at once, holding the harmonica on a brace around his neck.

UNDERNEATH THE LAMPLIGHT, BY THE BARRACKS GATE··· DARLING I REMEMBER, THAT'S WHERE YOU USED TO WAIT."

He also told the best stories. When I was a tiny little girl and still afraid of the stars, he sometimes took me for walks at night and told me long magical stories of the origins of the stars and of the many gods who created the universe. My father's made-up mythology is still much more interesting than the stories the scientists have invented.

When I had to have braces on my teeth, for nine years, my father drove me into the city to the orthodontist every Saturday morning. I'm sure he would much rather have spent the time fishing the quiet backwaters that he loved, but for me, those city trips were journeys into a magical kingdom. Some Saturdays, after the dentist, I got to go to the Philadelphia Art Museum as a reward.

I should have been afraid of that grand, imposing building, but I wasn't. I loved it. I loved the vales and glades and corridors full of paintings, and the tapestries and glass and wood and furniture that the artists who had done the paintings must have used or known! Or at least thought about.

There's a little painting by Breughel in a corner of a hallway. It shows a fat man with red stockings, running, running. His hands are clutching at his hat and his satchel. He is running away from a hillside full of sheep! Why? There is a dark tree to the extreme right of the painting, and a bird perched on the only branch. A yellow sky. I could feel his fear. Why is the man so afraid? But then, if you look closely, there is a wolf in with the sheep, sneaking closer and closer. Oh no! He's really Little Red Riding Hood! Oh, Brueghel, I love you.

KLORAINE AND LACEY

About the time I started with the braces, I also acquired a little sister. She was named Karleen, and she was round and rosy with eyes that tilted up at the corners. I loved her dearly, even though I teased her a lot and we sometimes fought. Eventually, she became the main audience and accomplice for all of my imaginary kingdoms, complicated games and elaborate fantasies.

Mostly, we loved fairies. They were more real to us than anything we could really see. But then Karleen started asking for a real one. One night, the moon gave me an idea; I'd make a real fairy for her! I was so excited, I couldn't sleep at all for the next week.

I bought a tiny celluloid doll at the Five and Ten, and when I got it home, I looked at it carefully. Oh, despair. How to make this dumb thing into a fairy?

My mother gave me a piece of her long, red-gold hair, which I glued to the head. Better! I painted the eyes big and blue. Not bad. I tried making dresses from cheesecloth and pieces of scarves, but nothing looked right. Meanwhile, I had started leaving tiny notes on Karleen's pillow.

"TAKE OUR MESSAGE TO THE KING! AND DO NOT FAIL, THIS TIME!

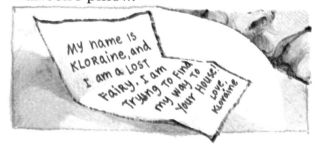

When Karleen found the first note, she was so happy and excited that she spoke in whispers the whole day. She believed it! If she did, then so must I. One day, after several tiny notes, I found a dead monarch butterfly on the ground at my feet. My father helped me take the wings off and glue them to Kloraine's shoulders. Oh, it was beautiful, and perfect! The next morning, Kloraine sat in all her splendor on Karleen's night table.

KLORAINE AND LACEY ARE LOST IN THE DEEP DARK FOREST!

Of course, Kloraine's butterfly wings splintered and disintegrated almost at the beginning of her adventures, and Lacey's big dark painted eyes faded into little mean punctuation marks. But the fairies stayed with us for many years and sat on the lowest, best branches of our Christmas tree even after we had both stopped believing in them.

Eventually, Lacey—another lost fairy—came to join Kloraine. Lacey was a tinier, sillier fairy. She had long red hair, too, and a lace dress, but I can't remember if she ever grew wings. She didn't need them, really. She was a sarcastic, argumentative, troublemaking fairy, who always made Kloraine's life more difficult and more exciting. Kloraine and Lacey had many exciting adventures in and around the weeping willow tree, and in the kitchen cupboards and the bathroom sink.

DO YOU REMEMBER WHEN THEY WERE LOST IN THE FOREST? HOW COULD I FORGET?

SCHOOL

Although I skipped first grade, I was a terrible student. I couldn't ever concentrate on what I was supposed to be learning about, because all I wanted to do was to be left alone, to read books or listen to music, or to draw pictures of witches and princesses when I should have been learning fractions. After eleven years, I came out of the public school system believing I was a hopelessly stupid little creature who would never be able to learn or to think.

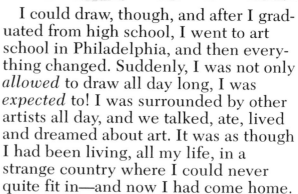

WHAT'S THE MATTER WITH YOU? ANSWER ME! DO YOU HAVE TO GO TO THE BATHROOM? ARE YOU READING IN CLASS AGAIN! WHY DO LOOK AT ME WHEN I'M SPEAKING TO YOU! IF I CATCH YC

I could draw, though, and after I graduated from high school, I went to art school in Philadelphia, and then everything changed. Suddenly, I was not only *allowed* to draw all day long, I was *expected* to! I was surrounded by other artists all day, and we talked, ate, lived and dreamed about art. It was as though I had been living, all my life, in a strange country where I could never quite fit in—and now I had come home.

After the first year of basic drawing, painting, printmaking and design classes, I majored in illustration. My best friend, Barbara, was an illustration major, too. Barbara and I went everywhere together; we'd walk all over the city, drawing everything we saw: people, streets, doorways, subways, trees, piles of trash. If we discovered a "new" street, we were as excited as if we'd found a new world. Whenever we had any free time, we'd walk to the art museum and wander through its miles of beautiful rooms and quiet corridors, looking at paintings and drawing from them. And every day for lunch, rain or shine, we went to Rittenhouse Square. We took our sketch books, hamburgers, coffee and a big box of saltines for the crowds of pigeons.

We were comrades; we were *artists*. Everything was exciting and beautiful, and we loved it all.

THE PIGEON LADIES: 1958

BOSTON

At the end of my third year at the Philadelphia College of Art, Harris Hyman and I decided to get married. Harris was a mechanical engineer; he was moving to Boston, where he'd gotten a job, and then he was going to Sweden to study mathematics. He wanted me to go with him. So I said goodbye to Philadelphia and went to Boston with Harris in his little sports car, ready for new adventures.

I went to art school for that year at The Boston Museum School of Fine Arts, right around the corner from our apartment. Harris and I made new friends, but I missed having animals. I longed for a cat or dog, but no pets were allowed in our apartment building. Then, one evening, Harris came home with two shiny black eyes and a pink nose with quivering whiskers peeking out of his pocket. It was a tiny gray and white mouse! One mouse led to another, so to speak, and soon we had forty-seven pet mice who scampered about the living room, chewed the edges of my drawings, and slept in Harris' gym shoes. Most of them were half wild and lived in the partitions, but some were as tame

THE NEW BABIES   1959

Now, all our belongings were in two small suitcases, one paint box, one portfolio, and one small steamer trunk. Our ship sailed at eight o'clock one night, and friends came down to the harbor with us to see us off. The sea and sky were still pink from the sunset, but the stars were out, too. The ship pulled away from the dock very quietly, and we waved and waved until our friends couldn't see us anymore, and then we watched them walk away toward the city.

as dogs and lived on my drawing board in a housing complex of toilet-paper rolls, tissue boxes, and cereal boxes. Mouseville!

Soon, it was summer, and time for Harris and me to leave for Sweden. We gave away all our dishes and furniture and pictures, and sent the original mommy mouse to Philadelphia, to live with my family. I cried bitter tears because we had to leave the others behind, but we couldn't catch them all, and even if we had, I'm sure my mother would have put her foot down at the idea of forty-seven mice.

TROLLS

Harris and I lived in one big room in a big old house on a tiny winding street in Stockholm. All the windows and a giant table were on one side of the room, and all the rest of the furniture was on the other. Our landlady was Fru Svensson. She was ninety-two years old and looked like a very tiny, jolly troll. Harris went to classes at the university and worked for IBM-Sweden part time, while I went to art school again.

That spring, I got my first real job, illustrating a children's book called *Toffe och den Lilla Bilen (Toffe and the Little Car).* I had been taking my portfolio around to publishers, trying to get illustration work, ever since Philadelphia. Every month or so I did new pieces, and then went the rounds again. This time, an editor named Astrid Lindgren liked what she saw and gave me a book to do. Of course, the text was in Swedish, so it took nearly as long for me to translate it as it did to draw the forty-six black-and-white illustrations. It was fun! I made the heroine look like my friend Barbara. I actually got paid the equivalent of $300, and I was now a published illustrator!

As summer approached and it was time for us to leave Stockholm, Harris and I planned an adventure. We hadn't had any time to see the country during our year of school and work, and now we wanted to travel.

We bought a big, blue tandem bicycle and two sleeping bags with the $300 I had made on *Toffe,* tried to get in shape by pedaling the tandem at least ten miles a day and doing 150 knee bends every morning.

SHOW OFF!

We set out on a rainy June afternoon, with only the tandem, our sleeping bags, two changes of clothes, two raincoats, a bar of soap, my eye make-up, two ball-point pens, a sketch book each, maps, and $600. Our immediate goal was to catch an overnight ferry that would take us to the island of Gotland, forty-five miles away. The mist came up, and the lights in farmhouse windows came on. I knew then that I wanted to go home, but I had no home to go to—and that is what adventures are all about.

THE HILL IN FISKETORPSPARKEN   1961

We rode that heavy old tandem bike 2,800 miles in two and a half months. We slept in caves with bats, in grassy fields with cows, in forests, in youth hostels, in farmhouses, and in castles.

THE STONE CIRCLE AT HAVANG

We pushed on through rain, sun, mist, glaciers, and moonlight just to get to the next town. We saw magic trees and standing stones, and heard the trolls murmuring to each other under the roots of ancient forests.

On the Fourth of July, we crossed the Hardanger Vidda, which is a mountain plateau 4,000 feet above sea level, at the top of the Norwegian Alps. It was snowing hard, and the wind was blowing against us so strongly that it stripped the skin from our bare hands and left us with bleeding knuckles. The Vidda is sixty miles long, and there is one, long, straight, narrow gravel road from one end to the other. Because it is a plateau above the timberline, it is absolutely flat, with nothing to break the cruel wind; not a house, not a gas station or even a crossroad. We had to do the sixty miles in one day or else die from the cold.

The wind roared in our ears and blew snow and dust into our eyes. When it stopped for a few seconds, there was absolute, frightening silence, and then we could see herds of reindeer like a mirage, silhouetted far away against a burning orange sky. Sometimes there were strange, incongruous piles of boulders, where the old, buried trolls had had their Midsummer Night feasts. If we stopped to shelter against those rocks, we heard the trolls' wild laughter and felt their desperate, ancient sorrow, so after a while we left them alone.

All of a sudden, there in the snow and the wind was a hand-painted wooden sign. It said PEA SOUP. Off to the side, there was a little wooden house on stilts. When we went into the house, it was so warm that Harris's glasses steamed up. There were long tables of scrubbed white pine, embroidered curtains at the window and pine needles on the floor. The whole place smelled of fresh coffee and yeast and bacon. A solemn young girl with rosy cheeks, forget-me-not eyes and heavy, long blond braids came to meet us. She was wearing the old, traditional dress for Norwegian girls. Her feet were bare, and she carried two big wooden bowls of hot pea soup in her hands. Snow White!

We ate the pea soup, with big pieces of flat bread and sweet butter, and asked for more. We got it. We asked for schnapps, and we got that, too. Then we went out into the cold wind and rode the reluctant tandem for another hour. Suddenly, without warning, the plateau ended.

Before us lay a green and cozy valley
with a pink river running through it.
Old stone bridges crossed the river, and
orange lights shone from the windows
of houses. A few cows grazed, and we
could hear barking dogs and children's
voices calling clearly in the twilight.
Look—a short downhill walk, that's all.

After that, we bicycled easily through
Scotland and England, until finally the
old blue tandem died. When we had
$1.75 between us, we flew home from
London and arrived in New York City at
three o'clock in the morning. Two weeks
later, we were back in Boston.

1962 N° 1 LYNDEBORO PLACE

BOSTON, AGAIN

This time, we bought a little house. A very old, cramped, tiny house on a courtyard, right in the heart of downtown Boston, just two blocks from the Common. Most of that crazy, funny neighborhood is torn down now, replaced by a Howard Johnson's Motor Inn and a medical center. But the little house, amazingly, is still there.

It was a mess when we bought it, and we worked hard to fix it up. In between tearing down walls and sanding floors, I got the old portfolio out and went looking for work. Nobody seemed to want a young genius illustrator, but I was pretty tough in those days, and my determination was fierce. Eventually I did get work—two Little Golden Books and some textbook illustration. Not enough! I wanted to illustrate my beloved fairy tales, folk tales, and important, exciting children's books.

Just about then, an art school friend of mine got the job of art director for adult books at Little, Brown and Co. Wonder of wonders, she had a book that needed illustrating—a book of Irish folk tales—and she offered the job to me! It was an important favor in more ways than one. Because of the work I did on that book, another person at Little, Brown—Helen Jones, the children's book editor, whom I had pestered often and thoroughly with my portfolio—decided to give me a book to do, too. That was the start of the most important relationship of my professional life and an important friendship, as well.

I guess every young artist needs a special someone—a teacher, a patron, a relative, a friend, or an editor—who will say, "I believe in you. Call me if you need help, but I know you can do it." I loved and respected her with all my heart and listened to her carefully and learned a lot. She gave me courage and knocked some good sense into me at the same time.

Now that I was beginning to get real work, I was pregnant with more than the ambition to illustrate books. I was going to have a baby. I had visions of a shy, little pink-fairy daughter who would stand by my drawing board and keep me company.

Katrin Hyman was born, screaming her head off, in 1963. She didn't stop screaming, ever, for a year and a half, until she learned to talk. A shy little fairy she certainly wasn't; I never saw a more stubborn, aggressive, opinionated baby in my whole life.

For as long as Katrin, Harris and I lived there, the little house in Boston was always full to the brim with friends and parties, stray cats and frantic activity. Harris and I rode our beautiful new English bicycles everywhere, and Katrin rode on the back of mine. But I was restless and sad. I wanted to be an artist again. I wanted to move to a house in the country. Instead, we sold the house and moved to New York City, where all the action was.

THE STONE HOUSE

New York was a bad move and a bad dream. Nothing worked out as we had planned, and everyone was dreadfully unhappy. The city seemed like a prison to me. Eventually, Harris and I got a divorce, and Katrin and I packed up and escaped to the country. We rented a little old stone house on the northern banks of the Connecticut River in the village of Lyme, New Hampshire. Inside, the low-ceilinged rooms were filled with river-reflected light, and there was a big sun-washed room to use for a studio. Outside there were grassy fields full of wildflowers, cornfields, and cow pastures. There were sugar maples and birches and pine forests on the hills. Nancie, my painter friend from Sweden, and her two-year-old twin daughters, Clea and Gaby, shared the house with us.

"WHERE ARE YOUR MITTENS?"   "IN MY POCKET."

That winter, Katrin started nursery school in the town of Thetford, across the river. For fun, I wrote a little story about her called *How Six Found Christmas* and gave it to our landlord, Ed, as a birthday present. Helen Jones saw the story and liked it well enough to publish it. So now I was an author as well as an illustrator!

During the next five years, I worked harder than I ever had before. With two adults and three children, bills piled up, and although I was getting more and more work to do, there were still many months when there wasn't enough money for groceries. Nancie tried desperately to sell her paintings and then to get illustration work, both without success. Finally, we worked out a system so that I could take on more books, with Nancie doing the layouts and color overlays. We worked long, late hours at our drawing boards, but we were more secure now and happy. Friends came to visit from New York, Boston, Philadelphia, and even California; our lives were exciting and full of picnics and adventures.

Katrin, Clea and Gaby were all in school and growing up fast. Actually, we were all growing up in different ways. We acquired new strengths, new ideas, new cats, and Jessie, the dog. The little stone house was bursting at the seams, so Nancie and I went looking for a larger house to buy, stubbornly ignoring the fact that we had no money to buy it with. After nearly a year of looking at all the houses for sale in Vermont and New Hampshire, we found the house we were looking for right around the corner.

THE FARM

It was a big 150-year-old rambling gray farmhouse set back from the road on a little knoll. It had a scruffy, cheerful, comfortable look to it, like a weathered old New England farmer who might have seen better days, but certainly had no regrets. There were giant, mossy sugar maples in the front yard, weeping willow trees, tamaracs, lilac bushes, and a little stream running through the side yard. It had a woodshed, a barn, a stone wall, ancient apple trees, and a pond in the back field. It had fourteen rooms, three pantries, a big black woodburning stove in the kitchen, secret passageways, hidden doors, and lots of crazy little dormer windows.

It was love at first sight. I had to borrow so much money from the bank, from friends and from my mother that I had nightmares about it, but I bought the house. With the help of neighbors and friends, we moved our five years' collection of stuff out of the stone house and into the farmhouse on the coldest day of January. The next day, I set up my drawing board and went back to work.

One day in June, the publisher of a small Midwestern textbook company, his wife and two daughters came to see us at the farm. They wanted to start a magazine for children, and they wanted me to be the art director.

"That's crazy," I said. "I know absolutely nothing about being an art director!" "That's right," he said. "And we don't know anything about making a magazine either." She said, "We'll learn together." And so we did.

As the art director for "Cricket," I wrote to every illustrator whose work I'd ever admired or loved as a child or art student or envious fellow-illustrator. I also did some looking and found new artists whose work I liked and sent out the word that unknown and aspiring artists should send portfolios.

So, crash, bang! Nancie and I put together the first issue of "Cricket," cutting and pasting the galleys of type the editors had sent us, and finding pictures to go with the text. It was a clumsy, amateurish, strange little issue, but it had charm, and it worked. Over the coming months and years, the magazine got better and better, thanks to the help of the newly-hired designer—bearded, guitar-playing, daydreaming John Grandits, our new friend.

The following spring, Nancie and the twins left for California to seek their fortunes, and my friend Dilys came to share the house, my life, and the artists who were beginning to become part of "Cricket" magazine.

Artists came and went by letters, phone calls, taxis, drawings, and Volkswagens. The farmhouse glowed each Halloween with hundreds of jack-o-lanterns; each Christmas with candles and Christmas trees; each spring with flowers and sunlight, and each midsummer with a four-day party for all the artists who worked for "Cricket."

We gave wonderful parties and produced and directed an occasional fairy tale.

It was during those years that I did the pictures for *Snow White* and *Sleeping Beauty*.

Introduction: A Waltz

Katrin and Michael O'Donnell were waltzing. Gracefully, slowly, swiftly, turning with the wind, as people dance in a dream. They were ice skating on the pond, under a sky full of brilliant stars. The winter starlight shone on their flying hair: his white-gold and hers fire-black. They laughed, turned and swirled together. Katrin was wearing her silky panda nightgown, and Michael was wearing his best suit. It was forty degrees below zero and the stars came down one by one to waltz with them. I shook the snow from my boots and walked back to my drawing board.

Everything that I have told you is, of course, a fairy tale. Life is magical, after all. Nothing is safe and everything changes. The farm, however, stays somewhat the same. At least, so far. If you want to see how things are with me, look at the opposite page.

There is my good and dear friend Barbara talking with Katrin, who has just come home for a few days from Bennington College. And there is Mimi, my mother, to say hello to Katrin, but Hugh O'Donnell will stop her to talk about getting rid of those maple tree branches. Judith is the one sitting under the catnip, looking amused.

That's Betsy, bringing a basket of apples up from the cellar, and that's me with my head in the refrigerator. Sasha is waiting impatiently for whatever I come up with; Sam is sweetly in the way, and Maggie is outside barking her head off at Teddy (Hugh's dog), who she sees at least twice every day but still gets terrified at the sight of, and Mimi will praise Maggie for her bravery and good sense. Claudia, the cat, is smooching on Barbara's lap, and that's Lisl next to Sam, and Marty is peeking around the corner of the stove.

The phone is probably going to ring any minute. It will either be Harris or Muriel or John Grandits or Marianne Plummer, or else the editor wanting to know where this book has got to and do I think I can deliver it on time.

Later on, Barbara and I will take the
dogs for a walk around the pond.

There are more houses, more fences
and fewer trees now. Look back at the
farm; it is already disappearing into the
mist.

Let's go back, then. I've still got lots of
work to do. Come on, dogs, we're going
home.